Books in the 6 Tricks Series:

6 Tricks to Student NARRATIVE Writing Success
6 Tricks to Student PERSUASIVE Writing Success
6 Tricks to Student INFORMATIONAL Writing Success
6 Tricks to Student WRITER'S ORIGAMI Success

6 Tricks™
to Student
WRITER'S ORIGAMI Success ™

An Easy Guide for Students, Teachers & Parents

Mark Diamond
creator of
Writing to Command Attention!™ Workshops

illustrations by **Heather Knorr**

an **Anyone Can Write™** book

An Anyone Can Write Book
published in 2008

Anyone Can Write Books
2890 N. Hills Dr. NE
Atlanta, GA 30305

ISBN: 0-9771470-3-7
978-0-9771470-3-8

Illustrations: Heather Knorr

illustrations on pages 88, 91 and 93 by Jim Gilbert
all models traditional; origins uncertain

Dedicated to my Mother-In-Law
ORIGAMI MASTER DOROTHY KAPLAN

whose expertise, passion and boundless energy inspire
students of all ages from around the globe.

Dorothy's love of people, from all walks of life,
sets an example for each of us to emulate and cherish.

Thank you, Dorothy, for bringing the joys of folding to
thousands of willing and able hands, and thank you
for your help with the models in this book.

CONTENTS

Corner Pocket Bookmark

Desk Name Stand

Business Card Wallet

Snail Mail

The Snapper

Fool-Proof Proofreading™

CLEEB™

WHAT IS WRITER'S ORIGAMI™?

WRITER'S ORIGAMI is paperfolding used *before, during,* or *to complete* a writing lesson or project.

WRITER'S ORIGAMI provides **motivation** in the planning, sloppy copy, revising and proofreading steps in the **5** Steps of Writing.

WRITER'S ORIGAMI provides **reward** in the neat sheet step of the **5** Steps of Writing.

WRITER'S ORIGAMI is a catalyst for the development of creative writing projects and lessons.

WRITER'S ORIGAMI can also be used for multitudes of projects in non-language arts subjects, such as science, math, social studies, foreign language, music, art, ESL, PE and character education.

THE 5 STEPS OF WRITING

1. **PLANNING** (prewriting) – organize your writing

2. **SLOPPY COPY** (drafting, first draft, rough draft) – write your piece quickly; don't worry about the mechanics of writing

3. **REVISING** (make it great!) – add fascinating and unusual details; substitute special words

4. **PROOFREADING** – correct mistakes – spelling, grammar, punctuation, capitalization

5. **NEAT SHEET** (publishing, final copy) – copy it over neatly

The 6 Tricks

WAIT!

8 1/2 x 11

sharp & accurate creases

# of WRITER'S ORIGAMI

folding keywords

support writing projects

help thy neighbor

Trick 1

use **8 1/2 X 11** paper

Why waste time and effort cutting paper into required squares for traditional origami?

Instead, use ONLY 8 1/2 x 11 sheets, such as copy or printer paper.

All 6 Tricks Origami models have been chosen and designed for this sized paper.

use **FESTIVE-COLORED** paper

Brightly-colored paper motivates folders.

Reams of deep-colored printer paper with a variety of hues are available from office supply stores.

Trick 2

WAIT

to fold until each step is

EXPLAINED

and

DEMONSTRATED.

IT'S EASIER TO

FOLD AGAINST A HARD SURFACE

THAN UP IN THE AIR!

Trick 3

FOLD SHARP & ACCURATE CREASES

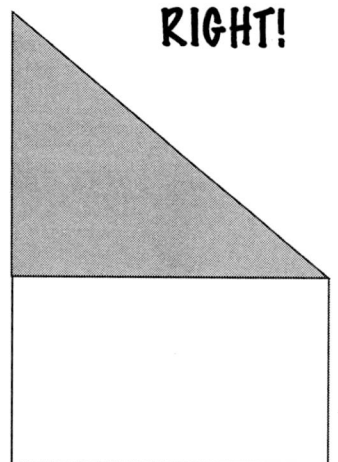

RIGHT!

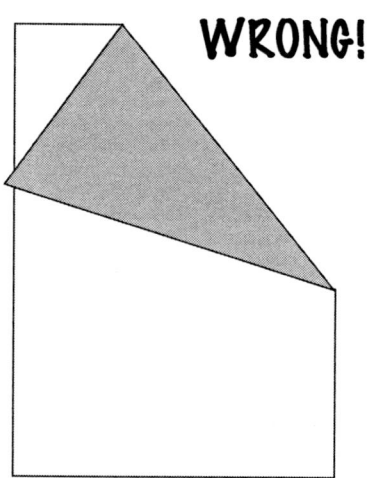

WRONG!

16

USE FLAT PART OF FOREFINGER NAIL TO CREASE FOLDS (while pressing with thumb)

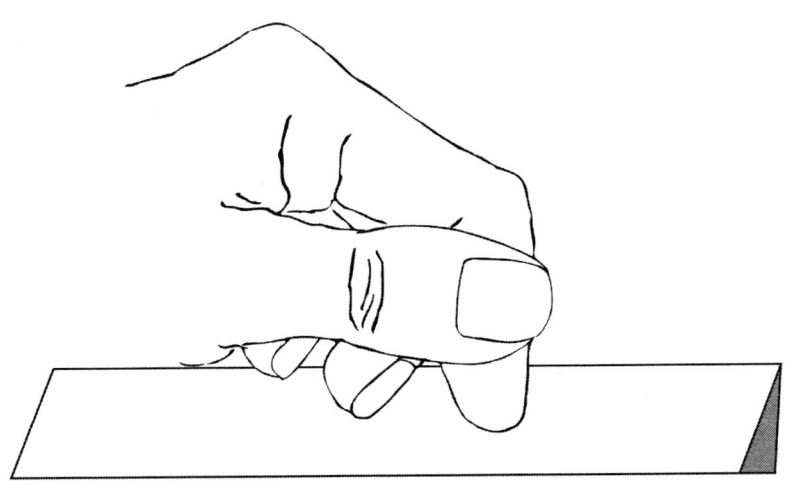

Trick 4

LEARN, USE & CREATE KEY WORDS & PHRASES FOR FOLDING STEPS

OPEN

HAMBURGER

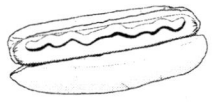

CLOSE

HOT DOG

CUPBOARD DOORS

AIRPLANE NOSE CONE FOLD

USE ORIGAMI MODELS TO BOOST WRITING PROJECTS

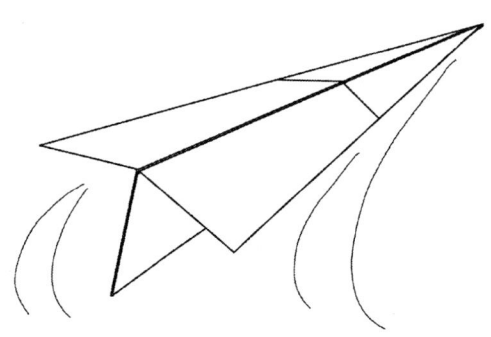

Get motivated with the excitement of a project that begins or includes folding an origami model and watch interest soar!

Trick 6

HELP THY NEIGHBOR

If someone's not getting it, others can help explain and demonstrate, but **SHOULD NOT PERFORM** the folds on a fellow folder's model.

ALL SET?

✔ Have 8 1/2 x 11 colored paper?

✔ Are all folders seated at desks or tables?

✔ Will this folding session serve as a reward, or either initiate or be included in a current project?

✔ Have folders been instructed to WAIT to fold until individual steps have been EXPLAINED and DEMONSTRATED?

OK then. Let's start!

BURRITO BOOK

2 sheets paper
scissors
pencil

STEP 1

**FOLD BOTH SHEETS
HAMBURGER**
(short side to short side)

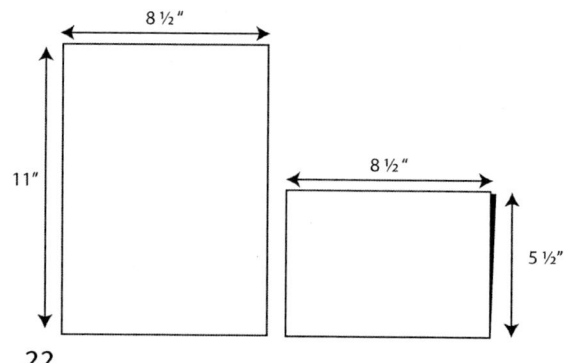

STEP 2

**ALONG FOLDED EDGES OF BOTH
SHEETS, USE PENCIL TO MAKE
SMALL MARKS 1 INCH AWAY
FROM LEFT AND RIGHT EDGES**

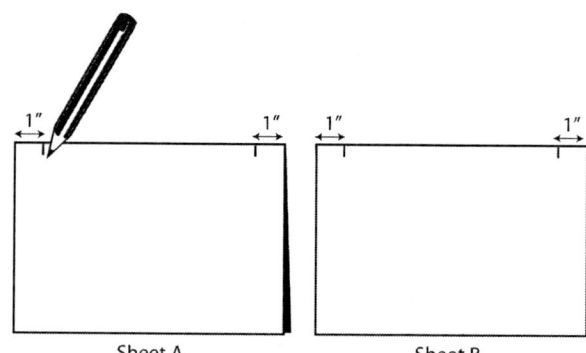

Sheet A   Sheet B

STEP 3

OPEN SHEET **A**

CUT ALONG FOLD FROM
EDGES TO PENCIL MARKS

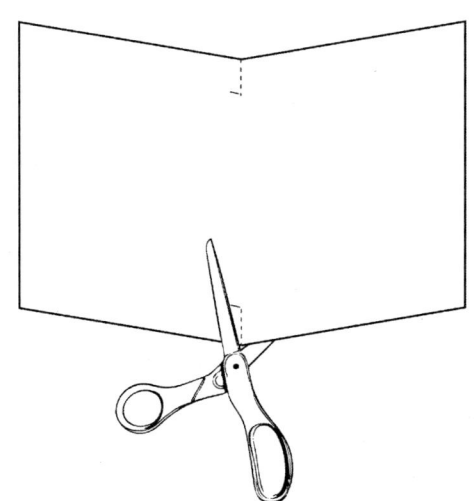

STEP 4

LEAVE SHEET **B** CLOSED

TRIM RIBBON OF SPINE
BETWEEN PENCIL MARKS

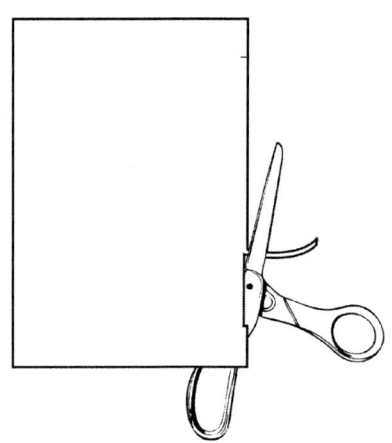

STEP 5

HOLD SHEET **B** OPEN HORIZONTALLY IN LEFT HAND

HOLD SHEET **A** IN HOT DOG FORMAT IN RIGHT HAND. IT SHOULD BE CURVED, NOT CREASED AT BOTTOM, LIKE A BURRITO

INSERT SHEET **A** (BURRITO) HALF-WAY THROUGH LARGE SLIT IN SHEET **B**

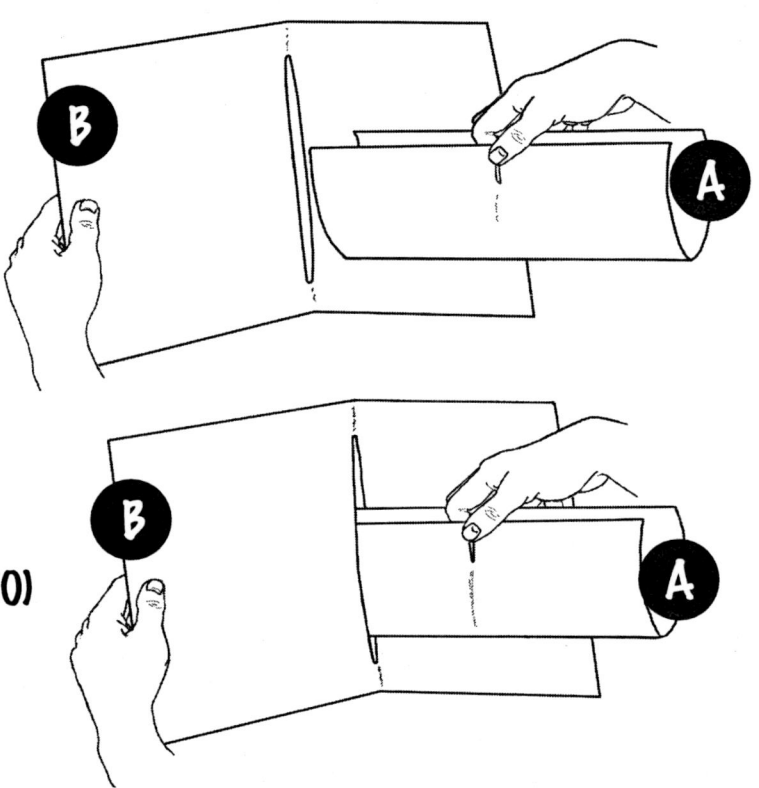

STEP 6

SLIDE *REAR* EDGE SLIT OF
BURRITO *UP*
TO ENGAGE SHEET **B**

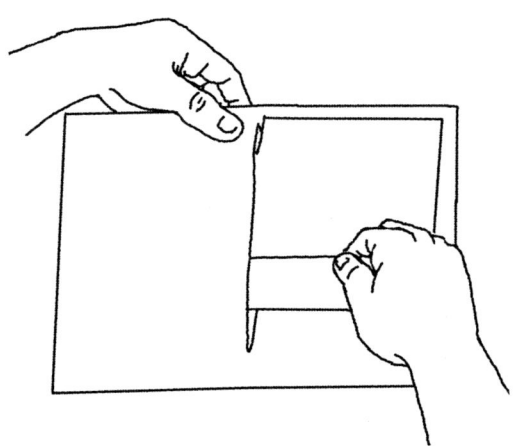

STEP 7

SLIDE *FRONT* EDGE SLIT OF
BURRITO *DOWN*
TO ENGAGE SHEET **B**

STEP 8

CLOSE BOOK AND RECREASE SPINE FOLD

If you want a burrito book with **LINED PAGES**, photocopy sheets **PRIOR** to folding.

You can download the lined sheet docs from **RESOURCES** at www.anyonecanwrite.com

For a Burrito Book of more than 8 pages, assemble with 2 or more sheets in each hand.

BURRITO BOOK STEPS REVIEW

hamburger both sheets
1 inch marks both sheets
edge cuts sheet A
spine trim sheet B
insert burrito into sheet B
slide top & bottom of burrito
           to engage
close book & recrease spine

BURRITO BOOK ACTIVITIES

tv guide narrative elements
family tree guide
world continents booklet
vocabulary guide
travel brochure
scientific method guide

 Get creative with cover art only AFTER ALL writing is finished.
Put Table of Contents on back side of front cover, to be completed
at END of project.

BURRITO BOOK TV GUIDE

AT THE END OF THIS WEEK-LONG PROJECT, WRITERS WILL BE FAMILIAR WITH THE ELEMENTS OF NARRATIVE.

✂ make Burrito Book together in class on Monday

✂ for each night of the week, choose one TV program and list the following info, under separate headings on one page of the book:

> ✂ name of program
> ✂ setting
>> ✂ time period in which story takes place
>> ✂ location of story
> ✂ plot summary
> ✂ character profiles; 3-5 sentences for each main character
> ✂ thumbs up? thumbs down? a brief critique of program

✂ complete one page per night for each of 6 nights
    (Monday-Friday plus one weekend night)

✂ back side of front cover should be left blank for Table of Contents

✂ at the beginning of the next week in class, the Table of Contents can
    be written, to include page numbers and the program titles
    from each page

✂ cover artwork can now be drawn

If you don't watch TV, profile any book, movie, theater
presentation, computer role-playing game (RPG)
or TV show you have EVER seen.

BURRITO BOOK FAMILY TREE

THIS PROJECT PROMOTES RESEARCH AND COMMUNICATION WITH FAMILY MEMBERS.

TABLE OF CONTENTS

1. _____
2. _____
3. _____
4. _____
5. _____
6. _____
7. _____
8. _____

2

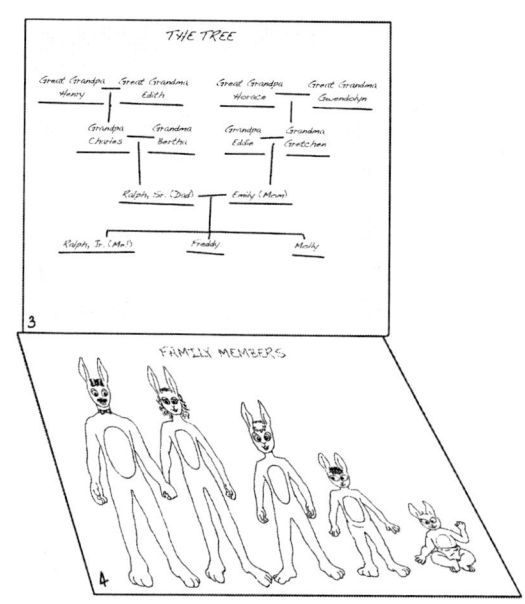

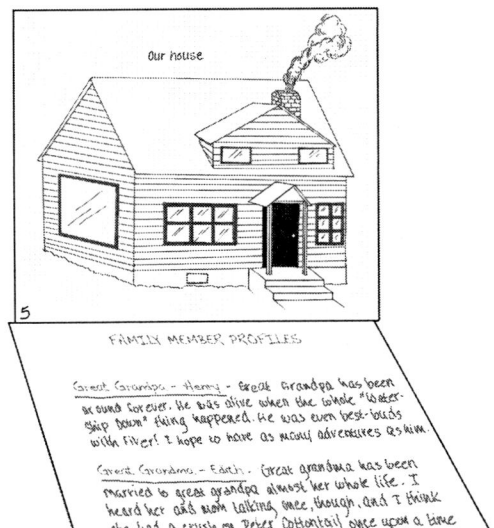

Our house

5

FAMILY MEMBER PROFILES

Great Grandpa - Henry - Great Grandpa has been around forever. He was alive when the whole "Watership Down" thing happened. He was even best-buds with Fiver! I hope to have as many adventures as him.

Great Grandma - Edith - Great grandma has been married to great grandpa almost her whole life. I heard her and mom talking once, though, and I think she had a crush on Peter Cottontail once upon a time. She loves grandpa more and wouldn't trade him for anything!

6

FAMILY MEMBER PROFILES - continued

Grandpa Charles - Grandpa Charles loves to tell stories about the old days. He's really funny. He said he had to hop to school in the snow, uphill, both ways! I know it couldn't be both ways!

Grandma Bertha - Grandma Bertha is quiet. Guess she has to be since grandfather talks so much. She's really nice, though, and everyone loves her. She can find the best cabbage this side of the country.

DAD - Ralph Sr. - I have the greatest dad in the world. He taught me to respect my elders and be kind to those who are younger. Best of all, he taught me how to find the biggest carrots!

Mom - Emily - My mom used to be a beauty queen. She even won a trophy at a pageant. More importantly, she makes the best carrot cake and alfalfa greens in the whole world!

7

FAMILY MEMBER PROFILES - continued

Me - Ralph Jr. - What can I say? I'm me and I love my family and Mr. D!

Little brother - Freddy - He asks a lot of questions sometimes, but Dad says he's just inquisitive and I was the same way. He's a good kid, though, and we have fun together. He can hop really far!

Baby Sister - Molly - Molly is newest to our family. She doesn't cry much, but she giggles all the time. She makes everyone laugh. She's funny.

8

Family member profiles on pages 6-8 contain at least 3 sentences of interesting information about people on the family tree.

MINI-REFERENCE BOOK

1 sheet paper
scissors

STEP 1

HAMBURGER
(1/2 fold)

STEP 2

HAMBURGER
(1/4 fold)

STEP 3

HAMBURGER
(1/8 fold)

STEP 4

OPEN TO 1/2 FOLD

STEP 5

STARTING AT FOLDED EDGE, CUT ALONG CREASE AND STOP AT PERPENDICULAR CREASE

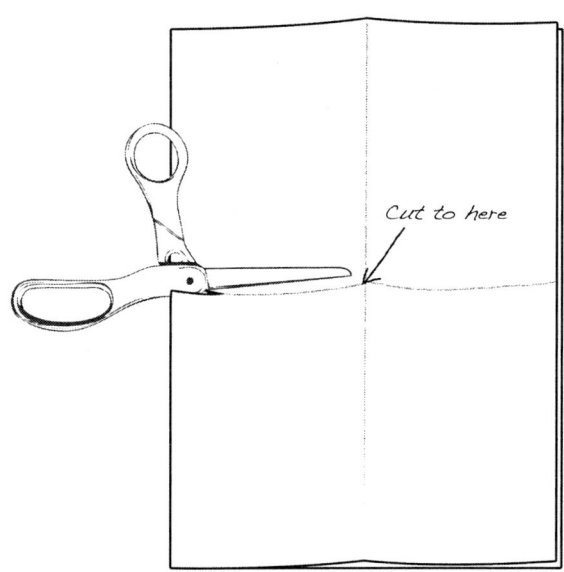

Cut to here

STEP 6

OPEN & FOLD HOT DOG
(towards you)

STEP 7

HOLD SHORT EDGES OF HOT
DOG IN FRONT OF YOUR FACE
& PUSH TOWARD CENTER
UNTIL YOU SEE A DIAMOND

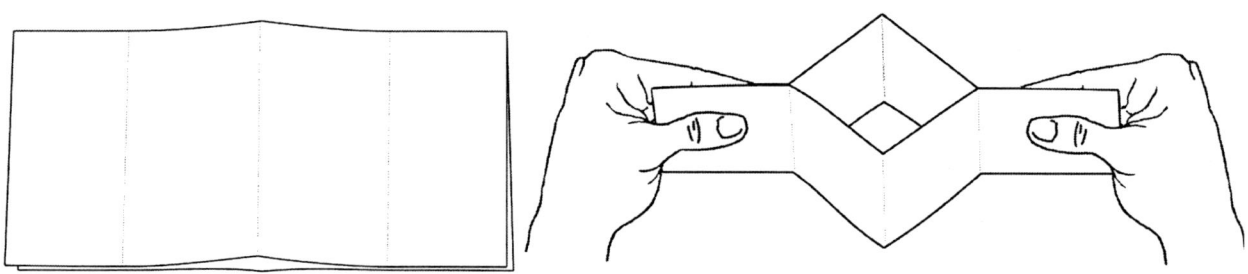

STEP 8

CONTINUE PUSHING TOWARD CENTER UNTIL THE DIAMOND IS ELIMINATED & THE PAGES LAY FLAT

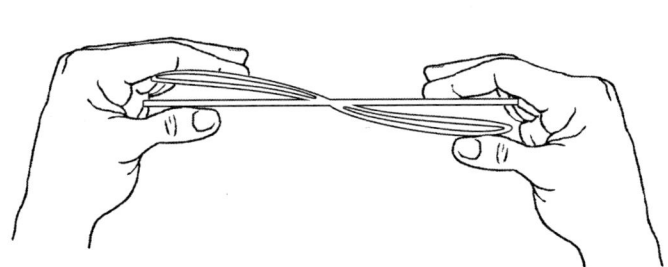

STEP 9

FOLD IN HALF & RECREASE THE 8-PAGE BOOKLET

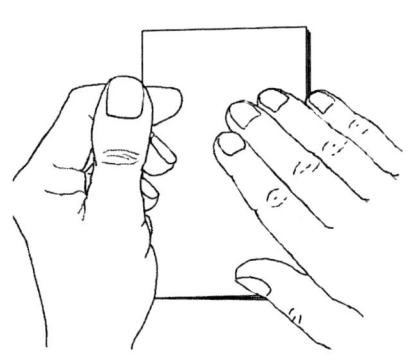

MINI-REFERENCE BOOK STEPS REVIEW

hamburger (1/2 fold)
hamburger (1/4 fold)
hamburger (1/8 fold)
open to 1/2 fold
cut along crease until fold
open and fold hot dog
eliminate diamond
recrease

MINI-REFERENCE BOOK USES

personal spelling guide
personal vocabulary guide
punctuation guide
grammar guide
math tables
math functions

MINI-REFERENCE BOOK PERSONAL SPELLING GUIDE

Do you spell the same words incorrectly over and over? Just list your troublesome words in this guide (with several letters of the alphabet on each page) and keep it in your desk or backpack for easy reference.

EFGH

effective
especially
embarrass

foreign
guarantee

guinea pig
grateful

height

IJKL

its / it's
kernel
library
license

AIR MAIL

1 sheet paper

STEP 1

WRITE NOTE OR LETTER ON ONE SIDE OF PAPER

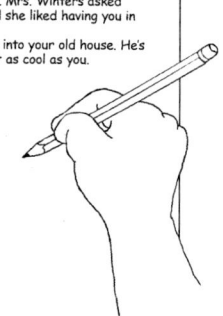

Dear Michael,

I was so glad to get your last letter. I'm glad you're doing well in your new home. We have been working on a lot of new stuff in class. It's been fun. Mrs. Winters asked about you. She said she liked having you in our class.

A new kid moved into your old house. He's pretty cool, but not as cool as you.

STEP 2

FOLD LETTER HOT DOG WITH WRITING INSIDE

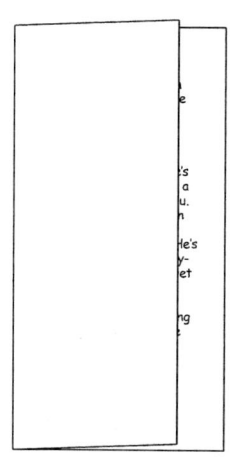

STEP 3

OPEN

Dear Michael,

I was so glad to get your last letter. I'm glad you're doing well in your new home. We have been working on a lot of new stuff in class. It's been fun. Mrs. Winters asked about you. She said she liked having you in our class.

A new kid moved into your old house. He's pretty cool, but not as cool as you. He has a set of tonka trucks that would surprise you. I never saw so many. All the kids get out in that old lot down the street and play with his trucks until our parents call us home. He's a pretty friendly kid and shares with everyone. His name is Buster. I'm sure you will get to meet him when you come to spend the summer next week.

Bring your swimsuit. Mom says we're going to spend a few days at the lake. Maybe we can bring Buster along, too.

See you soon!

Your friend,
Ralph

AIRPLANE NOSE CONE FOLD
fold top corners into right triangles against center crease

your last letter. I'm
your new home. We
lot of new stuff in
s. Winters asked
liked having you in

A new kid moved into your old house. He's
pretty cool, but not as cool as you. He has a
set of tonka trucks that would surprise you.
I never saw so many. All the kids get out in
that old lot down the street and play with
his trucks until our parents call us home. He's
a pretty friendly kid and shares with everyone. His name is Buster. I'm sure you will get
to meet him when you come to spend the
summer next week.
   Bring your swimsuit. Mom says we're going
to spend a few days at the lake. Maybe we
can bring Buster along, too.
   See you soon!

Your friend,
Ralph

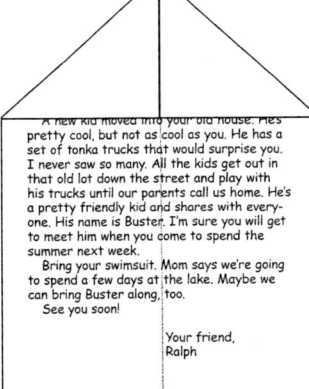

A new kid moved into your old house. He's
pretty cool, but not as cool as you. He has a
set of tonka trucks that would surprise you.
I never saw so many. All the kids get out in
that old lot down the street and play with
his trucks until our parents call us home. He's
a pretty friendly kid and shares with everyone. His name is Buster. I'm sure you will get
to meet him when you come to spend the
summer next week.
   Bring your swimsuit. Mom says we're going
to spend a few days at the lake. Maybe we
can bring Buster along, too.
   See you soon!

Your friend,
Ralph

STEP 6   STEP 7

CUPBOARD DOOR FOLDS
fold left and right sides to center crease

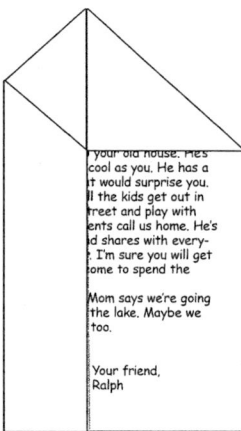

your old house. He's
cool as you. He has a
it would surprise you.
ll the kids get out in
treet and play with
ents call us home. He's
d shares with every-
. I'm sure you will get
ome to spend the

Mom says we're going
the lake. Maybe we
too.

Your friend,
Ralph

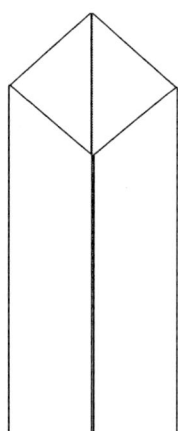

STEP 8

FOLD TOP OF DIAMOND
TO BOTTOM
OF DIAMOND

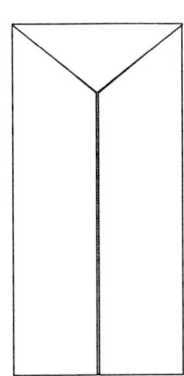

STEP 9

FLIP TOP OF
DIAMOND BACK UP

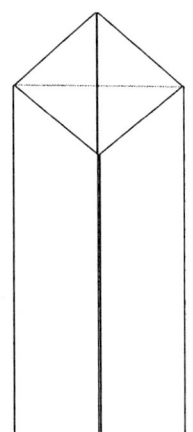

STEP 10

FOLD BOTTOM OF LETTER
UP TO CREASE IN
DIAMOND

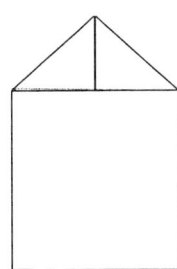

STEP 11

CLOSE ENVELOPE BY INSERTING DIAMOND FLAP INTO POCKET UNDERNEATH FLAP, THEN TURN OVER

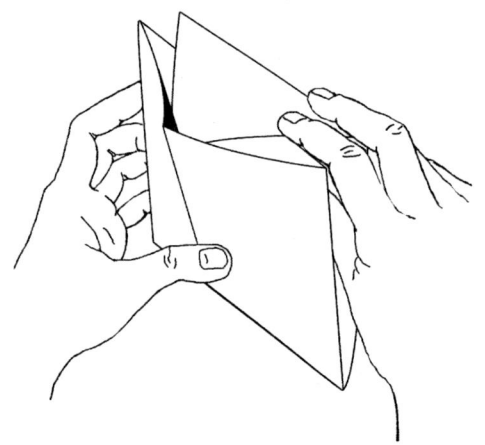

STEP 12

IF SENDING THROUGH THE U.S. MAIL, PLACE A DECORATIVE SEAL WHERE FLAP IS INSERTED INTO POCKET, ADDRESS THE FRONT, STAMP & MAIL

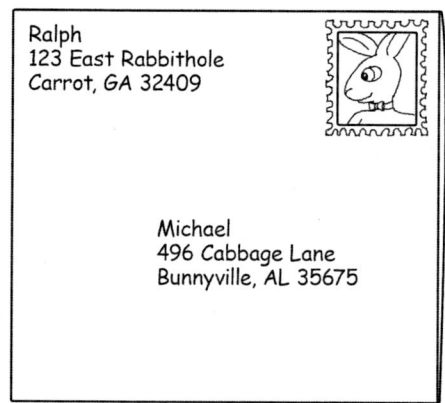

Ralph
123 East Rabbithole
Carrot, GA 32409

Michael
496 Cabbage Lane
Bunnyville, AL 35675

AIR MAIL STEPS REVIEW

write letter
hot dog
open
airplane nose cone
cupboard doors
top diamond to bottom diamond
flip top back up
bottom up to diamond crease
flap into pocket
tape, address & mail

AIR MAIL ACTIVITIES

notes/letters within school
notes/letters to go home
notes/letters sent through U.S. Mail
  to writers, entertainers & athletes
secret ballots

for learning the 6 Parts of a Letter:
  Heading
  Greeting
  Body
  Closing
  Signature
  P. S.

PICTURE FRAME

1 sheet festive paper

STEP 1

HOT DOG

STEP 2

OPEN

STEP 3

CUPBOARD DOORS

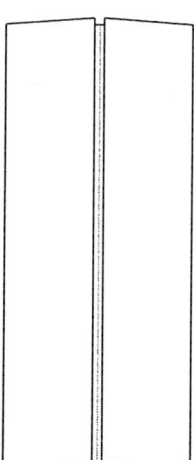

STEP 4

OPEN

STEP 5

FOLD EACH CORNER INTO A RIGHT TRIANGLE WITH ONE SIDE AGAINST NEAREST CREASE

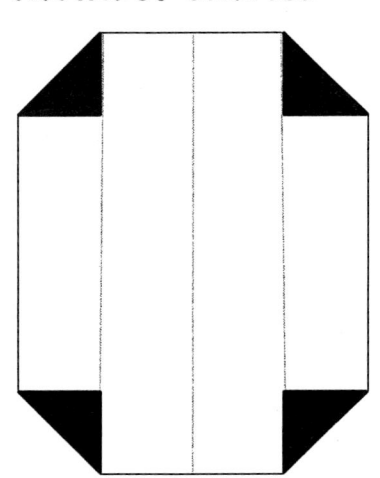

STEP 6

CLOSE CUPBOARD DOORS & RECREASE WITH CORNER FOLDS TUCKED INSIDE

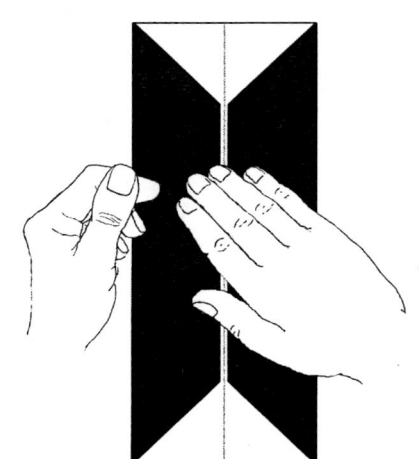

STEP 7

TURN OVER & LAY
CUPBOARD DOORS SIDE
DOWN ON FLAT SURFACE

STEP 8

BEND SHORT SIDES UP TOWARD
EACH OTHER AND INSERT ONE
SHORT END INTO THE POCKET OF
THE OTHER SHORT END TO CREATE
THE ADJUSTABLE PICTURE FRAME

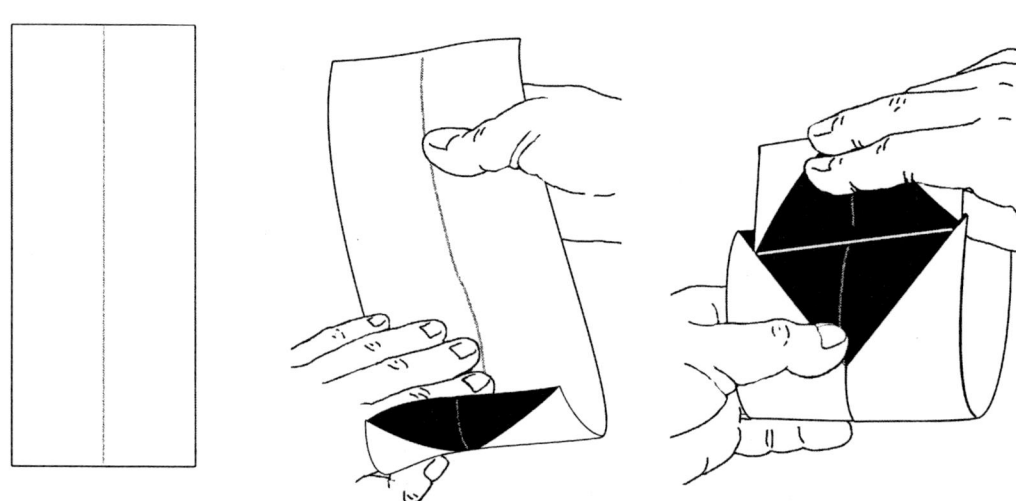

STEP 9

CUSTOMIZE THE PICTURE AREA BY SLIDING ENDS FARTHER IN OR OUT

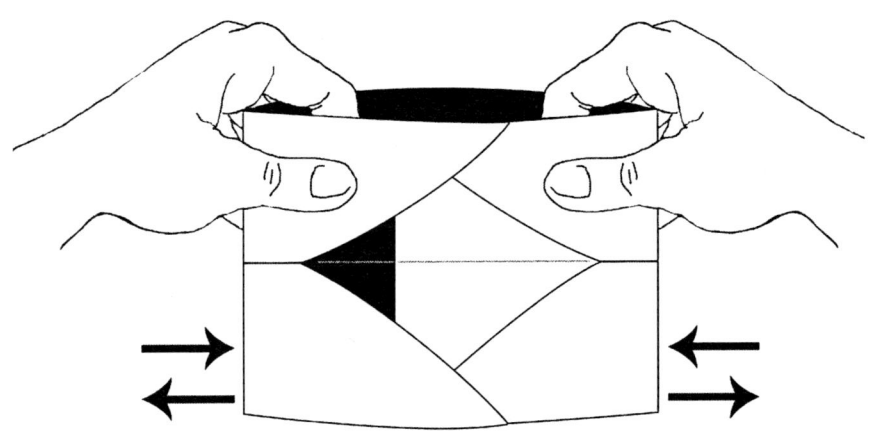

 Don't flatten yet! See next pages for display suggestions.

3 WAYS

WRIST FRAME

DESK FRAME

GLUE OR TAPE BACK OF
PHOTO INSIDE FRAME

to DISPLAY

FLAT FRAME

front   back

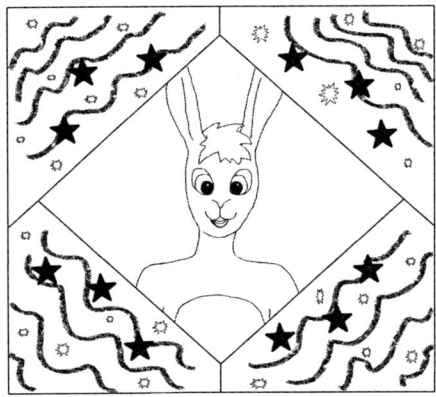

Dear Mom,
  A carrot, a card,
  some cake and tea
  The only thing missing:
  a picture of
      ME!
          Love and xxxx,
          Ralph

DECORATE FRONT WITH MARKERS, GLITTER GLUE & STARS

WRITE GREETING OR POEM ON BACK

PICTURE FRAME STEPS REVIEW

hot dog

open

cupboard doors

open

corner folds

close doors & recrease

turn over

short end into short end
to adjust frame size

complete as wrist frame,
standing frame or flat
frame with greetings
and decorate

PICTURE FRAME ACTIVITIES

WALLET-SIZED CLASS PICTURE GIFTS

Birthdays
Mother's Day
Father's Day
Grandparent's Days
Christmas Tree
    ornament
Thank you notes

WRITING ON BACK MAY INCLUDE

Prose message
Poetry message
Top 5 or 10 lists
4-panel cartoon
Party/Event
    Invitation
Biographical info
Picture description

PROJECTS

Memoir pix
Biography pix
Travel package insert
Election promo
Poems about pix
    or drawing
    within frame

CORNER POCKET BOOKMARK

1 sheet festive paper

STEP 1

HAMBURGER
WITH
VERY SHARP CREASE

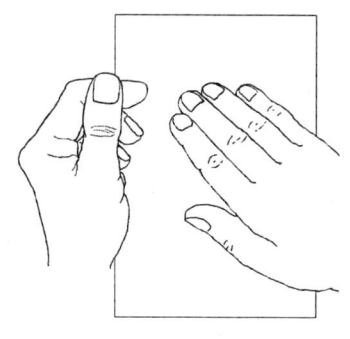

STEP 2

OPEN & CAREFULLY &
SLOWLY TEAR SHEET
IN HALF

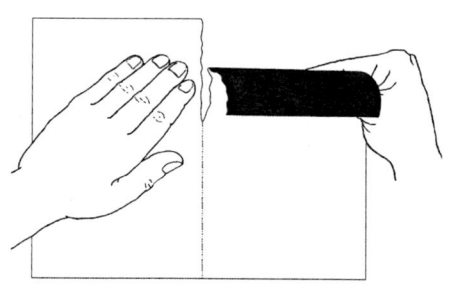

OR

STEP 3

CUT SHEET IN HALF

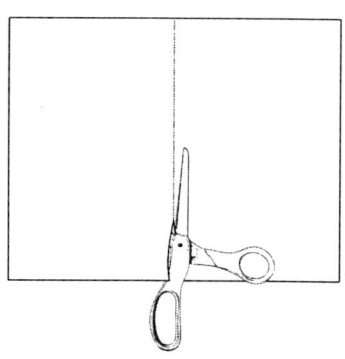

52

STEP 4

SAILBOAT FOLD
FOLD UPPER RIGHT CORNER DOWN DIAGONALLY TO MAKE A RIGHT TRIANGLE

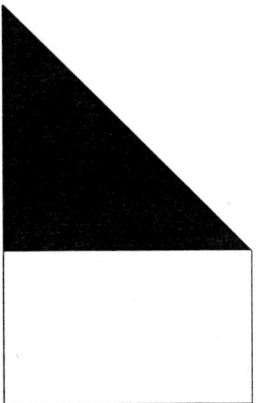

STEP 5

FOLD BOTTOM UP TO BOTTOM OF TRIANGLE

STEP 6

FOLD UPPER LEFT CORNER DOWN TO MEET TOP RIGHT EDGE OF RECTANGLE

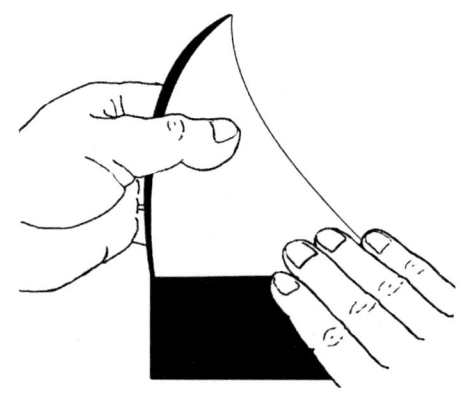

BEFORE

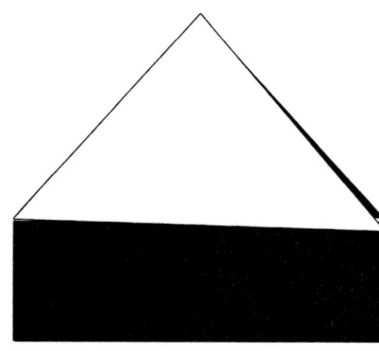

AFTER

STEP 7

FOLD BOTTOM CORNERS IN RIGHT-TRIANGLE FOLDS UP TO MEET CREASE

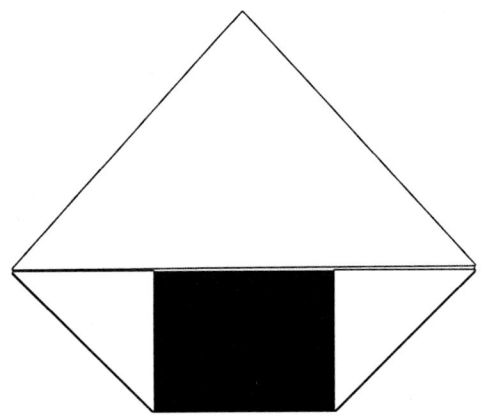

STEP 8

INSERT BOTTOM SECTION FLAP INTO POCKET OF UPPER SECTION TRIANGLE

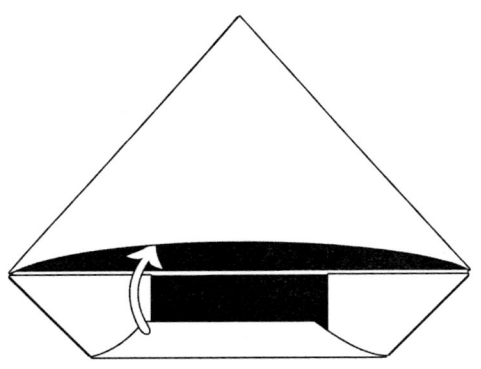

STEP 9

INSERT SEVERAL
PAGE CORNERS
INTO POCKET OF BOOKMARK
TO MARK YOUR PLACE

BOOKMARK STEPS REVIEW

make hamburger half sheet
sailboat fold
bottom up to sail
sail in half
bottom corner folds
flap into pocket

BOOKMARK ACTIVITIES

As you are reading, use the corner pocket bookmark to jot down the following:

quotes to remember
pages to note
facts of interest
new vocabulary words
character list
important dates
appealing phrases

DESK NAME STAND

1 sheet festive paper

STEP 1

HOT DOG

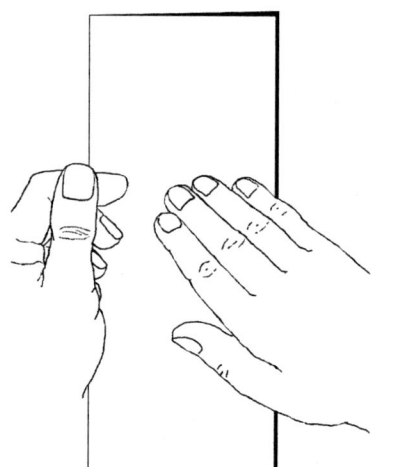

STEP 2

FOLD TOP LEFT CORNER
OF FOLDED EDGE DOWN
INTO RIGHT TRIANGLE

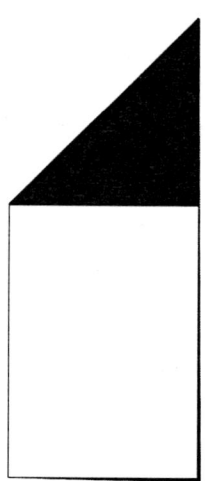

STEP 3

FOLD BOTTOM LEFT CORNER OF FOLDED EDGE UP INTO RIGHT TRIANGLE

STEP 4

FOLD LEFT TO RIGHT SIDE

STEP 5

ROTATE MODEL
COUNTER-CLOCKWISE
1/4 TURN (90 DEGREES)

STEP 6

FOLD DIAGONAL EDGES IN
FLUSH WITH BOTTOM

STEP 7

EXTEND SIDE & BOTTOM FLAPS FOR SUPPORT (REAR VIEW)

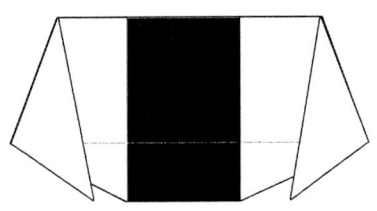

STEP 8

PRINT NAME NEATLY ON FRONT

Ralph

DESK NAME STAND STEPS REVIEW

hot dog
folded edge corners into right
    triangles
left to right side
rotate 1/4 turn
    counter-clockwise
diagonal edges flush
    with bottom
extend side and bottom supports

DESK NAME STAND USES

learn names of classmates at start
    of school year

panel discussion member IDs

identify displays

place cards for parties

write notes on back of cards

DESK NAME STAND EXAMPLES (BACKS)

IF THE #2 PENCIL IS SO POPULAR, WHY IS IT STILL #2?	TREAT OTHERS AS YOU WOULD LIKE TO BE TREATED	MONTHS THAT BEGIN ON A SUNDAY WILL ALWAYS HAVE A "FRIDAY THE 13TH"
WRITE GOALS EACH DAY CHECK THEM OFF AS YOU ACCOMPLISH THEM	DID YOU KNOW YOU SHARE YOUR BIRTHDAY WITH 9 MILLION OTHER PEOPLE IN THE WORLD?	DARE TO DREAM BUT PAY ATTENTION TO WHAT YOU'RE DOING

BUSINESS CARD WALLET

1 sheet festive paper

STEP 1

HOT DOG

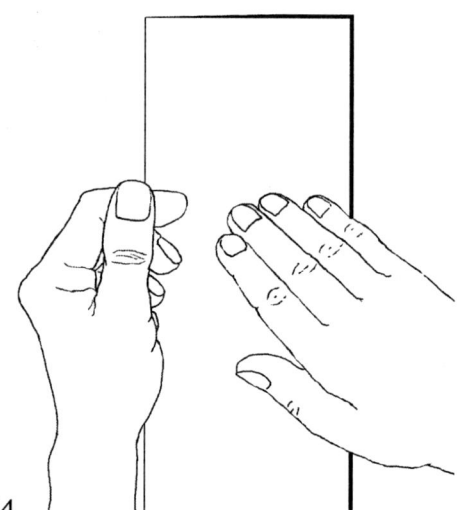

STEP 2

OPEN

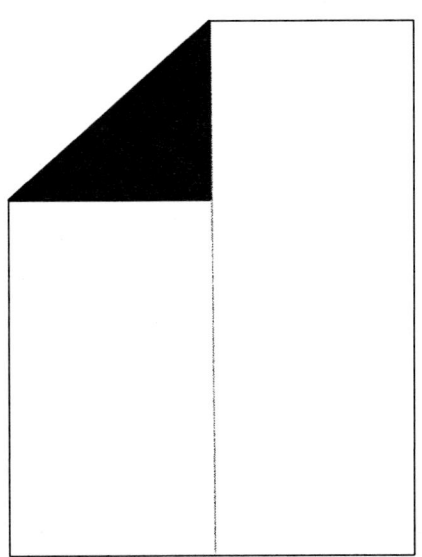 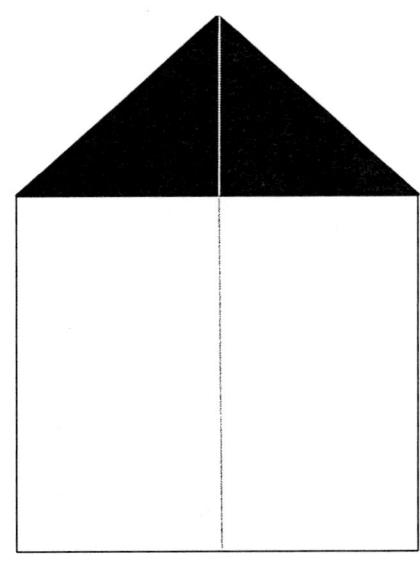

STEP 3

STEP 4

AIRPLANE NOSE CONE FOLD
fold top corners into right triangles against center crease

STEP 5

FOLD TOP POINT DOWN TO BOTTOM

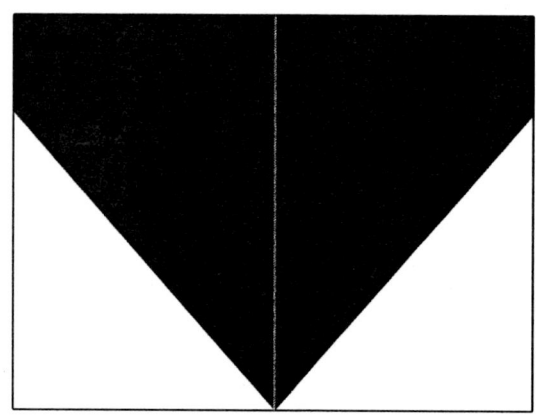

STEP 6

TURN OVER, MAKING SURE POINT IS STILL DOWN IN BACK

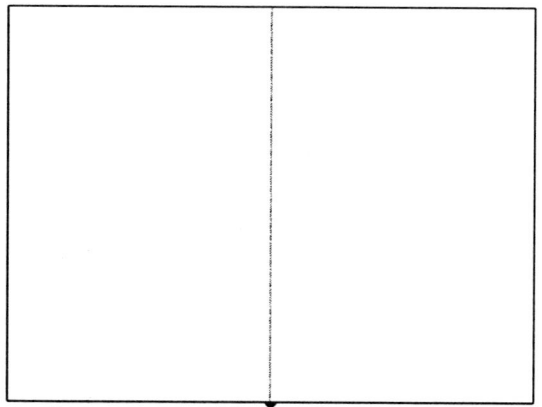

STEP 7 STEP 8

CUPBOARD DOOR FOLDS
fold left and right sides to
center crease & crease sharply

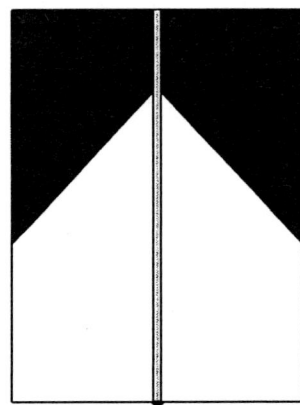

STEP 9

FOLD BOTTOM EDGE, BUT
NOT POINT, UP UNTIL IT
WILL GO NO FURTHER
WITHOUT TEARING &
CREASE VERY SHARPLY

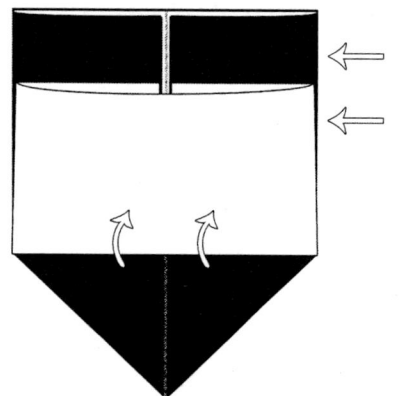

STEP 10

FOLD TOP FLAP DOWN OVER BOTTOM
FLAP AS FAR AS POSSIBLE WITHOUT
ADDITIONAL CREASING
OF BOTTOM FLAP
CREASE SHARPLY WITH PEN,
PENCIL OR COIN

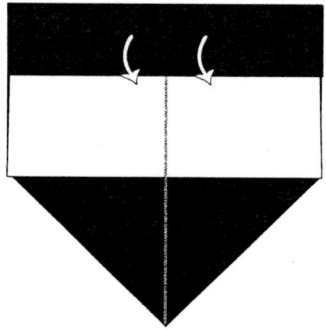

STEP 11

TUCK BOTTOM FLAP SECURELY INTO POCKET OF TOP FLAP

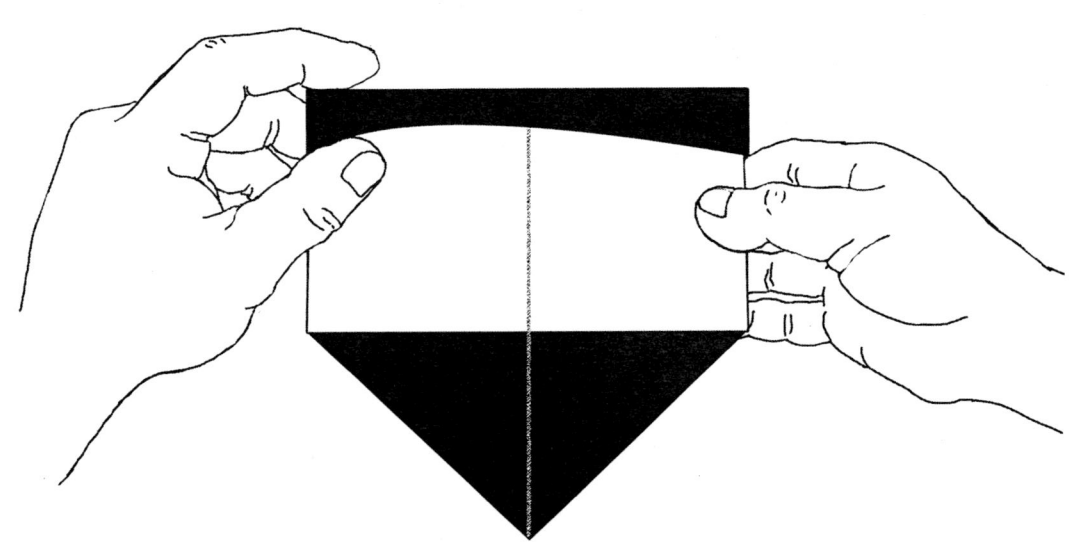

STEP 12

FOLD BOTTOM POINT UP &
INSERT UNDER TOP FLAP
TO CLOSE

STEP 13

TURN RIGHT SIDE UP, LIFT
CLOSURE FLAP & PLACE
CARDS OR OTHER ITEMS
INSIDE WALLET

BUSINESS CARD WALLET STEPS REVIEW

hot dog
open
airplane nose cone fold
top to bottom
turn over
cupboard door folds
bottom edge up
top flap down
bottom flap into pocket of top flap
turn right side up to use wallet

BUSINESS CARD WALLET USES

holder/container for:

business cards
paper money & coins
jewelry
stamps
paper clips
video game cards/carts

SNAIL MAIL

1 sheet paper

STEP 1

WRITE NOTE OR LETTER ON ONE SIDE OF PAPER

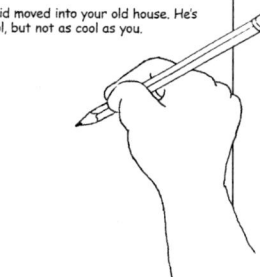

Dear Michael,

I was so glad to get your last letter. I'm glad you're doing well in your new home. We have been working on a lot of new stuff in class. It's been fun. Mrs. Winters asked about you. She said she liked having you in our class.

A new kid moved into your old house. He's pretty cool, but not as cool as you.

STEP 2

FOLD LETTER HAMBURGER WITH WRITING INSIDE

STEP 3

OPEN

Dear Michael,

I was so glad to get your last letter. I'm glad you're doing well in your new home. We have been working on a lot of new stuff in class. It's been fun. Mrs. Winters asked about you. She said she liked having you in our class.

A new kid moved into your old house. He's pretty cool, but not as cool as you. He has a set of tonka trucks that would surprise you. I never saw so many. All the kids get out in that old lot down the street and play with his trucks until our parents call us home. He's a pretty friendly kid and shares with everyone. His name is Buster. I'm sure you will get to meet him when you come to spend the summer next week.

Bring your swimsuit. Mom says we're going to spend a few days at the lake. Maybe we can bring Buster along, too.

See you soon!

Your friend,
Ralph

STEP 4

FOLD BOTTOM LEFT CORNER UP INTO RIGHT TRIANGLE AGAINST CENTER CREASE

Dear Michael,

I was so glad to get your last letter. I'm glad you're doing well in your new home. We have been working on a lot of new stuff in class. It's been fun. Mrs. Winters asked about you. She said she liked having you in our class.

A new kid moved into your old house. He's pretty cool, but not as cool as you. He has a set of tonka trucks that would surprise you. I never saw so many. All the kids get out in that old lot down the street and play with

l us home. He's
s with every-
re you will get
spend the

s we're going
e. Maybe we

STEP 5

FOLD TOP RIGHT CORNER DOWN INTO RIGHT TRIANGLE AGAINST CENTER CREASE

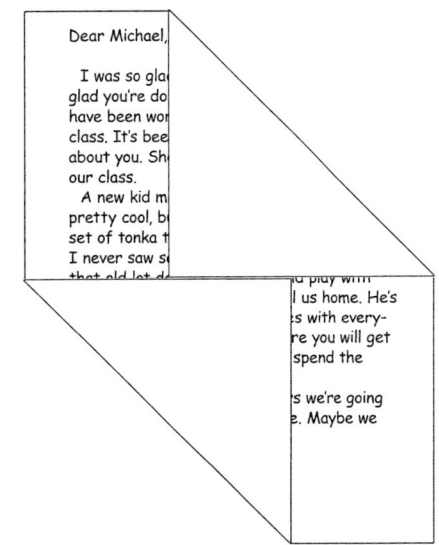

Dear Michael,

I was so glad
glad you're do
have been wor
class. It's bee
about you. Sh
our class.

A new kid m
pretty cool, b
set of tonka t
I never saw s
that old lot d

d play with
l us home. He's
s with every-
re you will get
spend the

s we're going
e. Maybe we

73

STEP 6

TURN HORIZONTALLY & FOLD BOTTOM OF LEFT SIDE RECTANGLE UP IN HALF TO MEET BOTTOM OF TRIANGLE

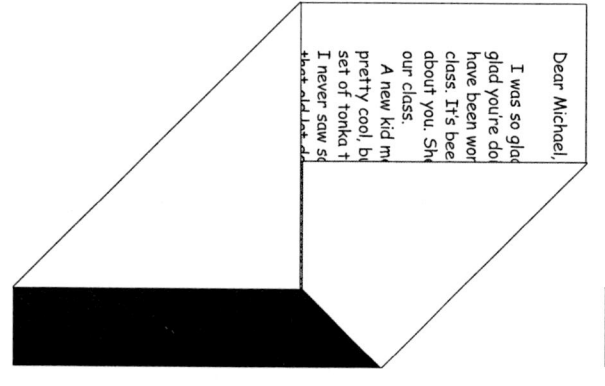

STEP 7

FOLD TOP OF RIGHT SIDE RECTANGLE DOWN TO MEET TRIANGLE, AS IN LAST STEP

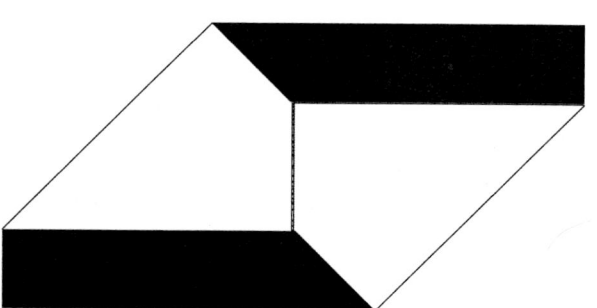

STEP 8

FOLD BOTTOM LEFT SIDE UP TO REST AGAINST CENTER CREASE

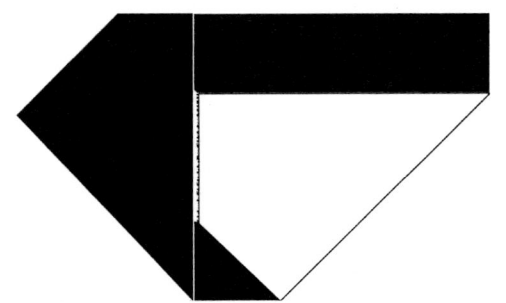

STEP 9

FOLD TOP RIGHT SIDE DOWN TO REST AGAINST CENTER CREASE

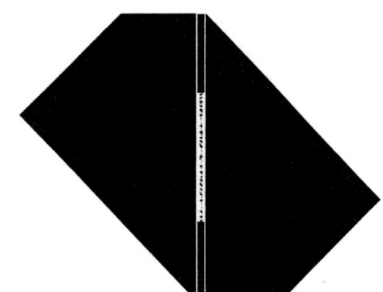

STEP 10

CLOSE ENVELOPE BY
TUCKING CORNER FLAPS
INTO POCKETS BENEATH
FLAPS, THEN TURN OVER

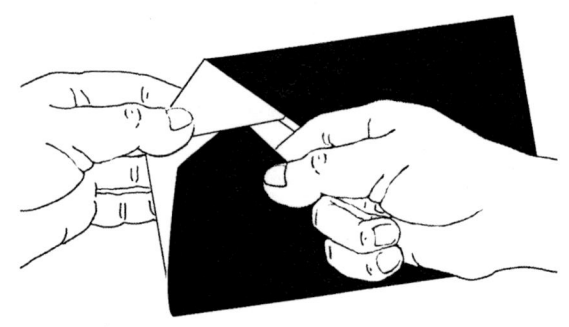

STEP 11

IF SENDING THROUGH THE U.S.
MAIL, PLACE DECORATIVE SEALS
WHERE FLAPS ARE INSERTED
INTO POCKETS, ADDRESS THE
FRONT, STAMP & MAIL

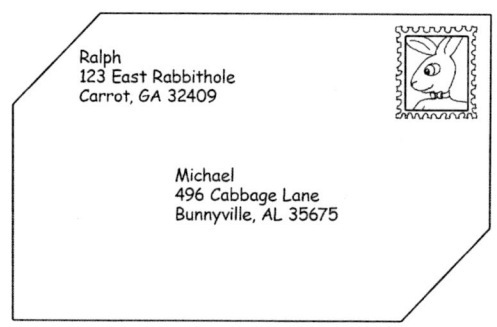

Ralph
123 East Rabbithole
Carrot, GA 32409

Michael
496 Cabbage Lane
Bunnyville, AL 35675

SNAIL MAIL STEPS REVIEW

write letter
hamburger
open
bottom left corner triangle
top right corner triangle
turn horizontally
rectangles in half
bottom left against center crease
top right against center crease
flaps into pockets beneath
tape, address & mail

SNAIL MAIL ACTIVITIES

notes/letters within school
notes/letters to go home
notes/letters sent through U.S. Mail
 to writers, entertainers & athletes
secret ballots

for learning the 6 Parts of a Letter:
 Heading
 Greeting
 Body
 Closing
 Signature
 P. S.

THE SNAPPER

1 sheet festive paper

STEP 1

HAMBURGER

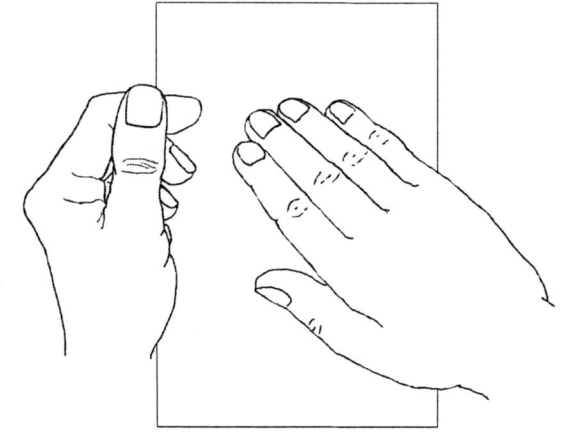

STEP 2

OPEN

STEP 3   STEP 4

CUPBOARD DOOR FOLDS
fold left and right sides to center line & crease sharply

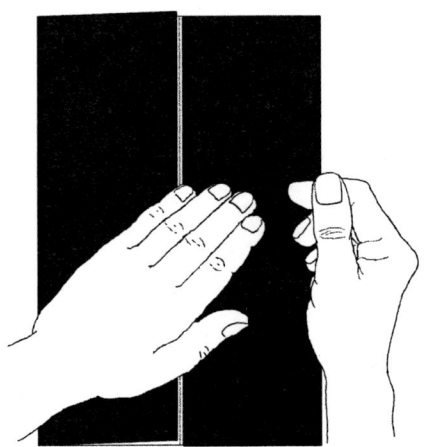

STEPS 5 & 6

CUPBOARD DOORS AGAIN! CREASE HARD!

STEPS 7 & 8

CUPBOARD DOORS YET AGAIN! CREASE HARDER!

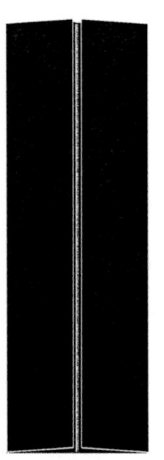

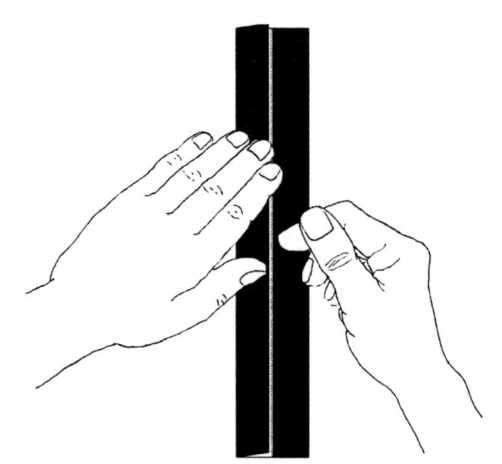

STEP 9

FOLD BOTTOM UP TO TOP
AND CREASE LIGHTLY

STEP 10

FOLD BACK DOWN AGAIN

STEP 11

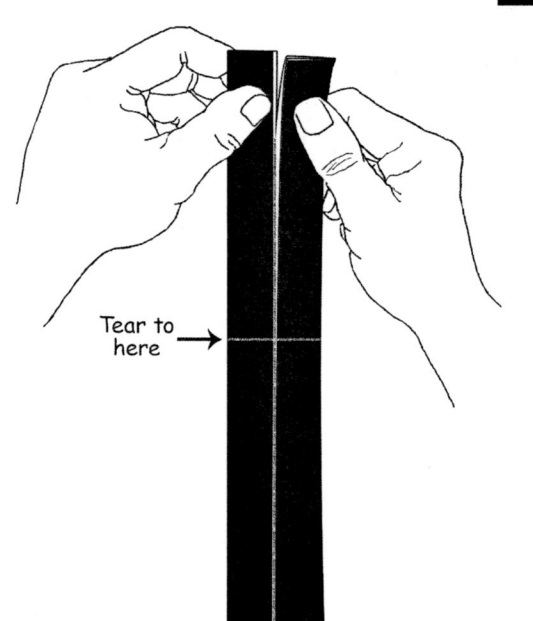

Tear to here →

STARTING AT TOP, USE THUMBS & FOREFINGERS TO CAREFULLY TEAR ALONG CREASE BY PULLING APART, THEN MOVING FINGERS DOWN & REPEATING UNTIL STOPPING AT LIGHT CREASE HALFWAY DOWN

STEP 12

FOLD IN ON ITSELF TO MAKE STICK

FOLD SIDES ALL THE WAY DOWN SO IT RESEMBLES A CHRISTMAS TREE

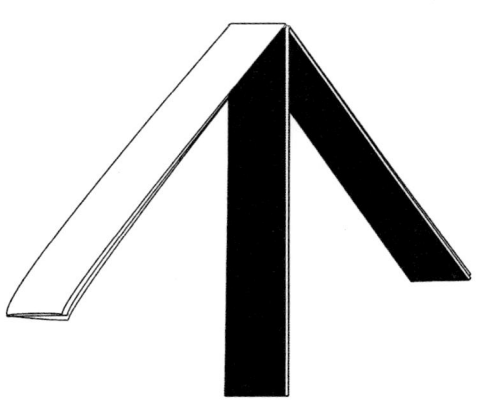

STEP 14

HOLD TREE AT BOTTOM WITH FINGERS OF YOUR LEFT HAND

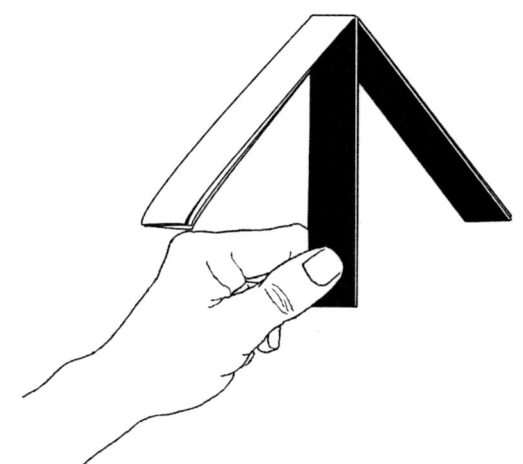

STEP 15

MAKE PEACE SIGN WITH YOUR RIGHT HAND

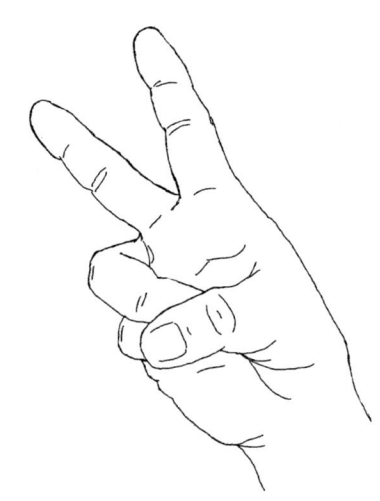

STEP 16

LIGHTLY PLACE PEACE SIGN FINGERS ON EITHER SIDE OF TREE BASE, JUST ABOVE LEFT HAND FINGERS

STEP 17

FLING PEACE SIGN FINGERS UP SWIFTLY TO SNAP!

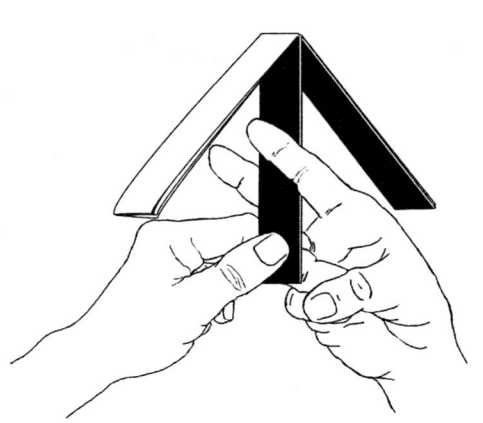

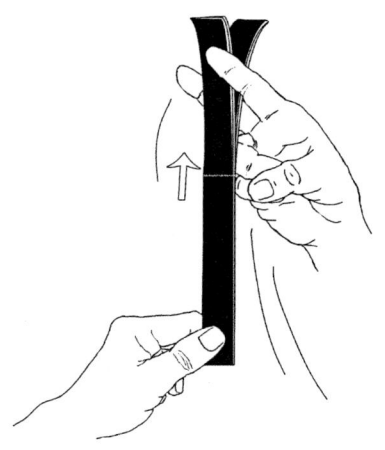

 Press tree sides down before repeating.

FOOL-PROOF PROOFREADING™

Silent proofreading does NOT work!

Peer editing is for practice only.

YOU MUST TAKE RESPONSIBILITY FOR YOUR OWN PROOFREADING!

A Proofread in a low voice so your ears can hear mistakes.

B Point to each word with your pencil as you say the word.

C Proofread in slow motion.

CLEEB™

5 Tips for Super Oral Presentations

Clear	**speak clearly**
Loud	**speak loudly**
Expression	**speak with feeling, like TV or movie actors**
Eye contact	sometimes look up from you paper to communicate with your eyes
Body movement	no leaning-stand up straight two hands on paper (gesture with one if needed) paper held at chest height

Now Get Out There and Write!

Don't Be Afraid to Make Mistakes!

The Only Thing You Can Do Wrong is Not Writing At All!

REVISE! REVISE! REVISE!

Meet Mr. D

Known to thousands of students as "Mr. D," Mark presents more than 300 seminars each year for elementary and middle school students, faculty and parents. His *Writing to Command Attention!* workshops merge learning with fun, providing lifelong skills in an entertaining package. Mark's narrative, persuasive and informational writing methods have been adopted by school districts across the USA.

E-mail Mr. D at Mark@AnyoneCanWrite.com or visit his website: www.AnyoneCanWrite.com

ORDER FORM

ORDER ON-LINE: www.AnyoneCanWrite.com

POSTAL ORDERS: Anyone Can Write Books
(check or PO only) 2890 N. Hills Dr. NE
Atlanta, GA 30305
Mark@AnyoneCanWrite.com

Please send me _____ copies of *6 Tricks to Student WRITER'S ORIGAMI Writing Success*
Please send me _____ copies of *6 Tricks to Student INFORMATIONAL Writing Success*
Please send me _____ copies of *6 Tricks to Student NARRATIVE Writing Success*
Please send me _____ copies of *6 Tricks to Student PERSUASIVE Writing Success*

1-9 copies @ $14.95 each   10-29 @ $12.95 each   30+ @ $10.00 each

School _____   Tax-Free ID # _____

Name _____

Address_____

City _____   State_____   Zip _____

Phone number   _____

E-mail address   _____

SHIPPING: $4.50 single copy; e-mail for multiple-copy shipping costs

NOTES

ORDER FORM

ORDER ON-LINE: www.AnyoneCanWrite.com

POSTAL ORDERS: Anyone Can Write Books
(check or PO only) 2890 N. Hills Dr. NE
Atlanta, GA 30305
Mark@AnyoneCanWrite.com

Please send me _____ copies of *6 Tricks to Student WRITER'S ORIGAMI Writing Success*
Please send me _____ copies of *6 Tricks to Student INFORMATIONAL Writing Success*
Please send me _____ copies of *6 Tricks to Student NARRATIVE Writing Success*
Please send me _____ copies of *6 Tricks to Student PERSUASIVE Writing Success*

1-9 copies @ $14.95 each   10-29 @ $12.95 each   30+ @ $10.00 each

School _____   Tax-Free ID # _____

Name _____

Address_____

City _____   State_____   Zip _____

Phone number   _____

E-mail address   _____

SHIPPING: $4.50 single copy; e-mail for multiple-copy shipping costs